The Sunflowers Babushka Planted

written by Beatrice Rendón illustrated by Olga Baumert

To Mom, Nana, Baba and the mamas and babushkas before you: Thank you for teaching us that resourcefulness and creativity beget resilience and hope. – BR

A note on pronunciation: "Babushka" means "grandmother" in many Slavic languages. To pronounce the word like the characters in the story would, say BOB-oosh-ka, with the emphasis on "BOB".

Raintree is an imprint of Capstone Global Library Limited, a company incorporated in England and Wales having its registered office at 264 Banbury Road, Oxford, OX2 7DY – Registered company number: 6695582

www.raintree.co.uk
myorders@raintree.co.uk

Text copyright © 2025 by Beatrice Rendón.
Illustration copyright © 2025 by Capstone Global Library Ltd.

The moral rights of the proprietor have been asserted. All rights reserved. No part of this publication may be reproduced in any form or by any means (including photocopying or storing it in any medium by electronic means and whether or not transiently or incidentally to some other use of this publication) without the written permission of the copyright owner, except in accordance with the provisions of the Copyright, Designs and Patents Act 1988 or under the terms of a licence issued by the Copyright Licensing Agency, 5th Floor, Shackleton House, 4 Battle Bridge Lane, London, SE1 2HX (www.cla.co.uk). Applications for the copyright owner's written permission should be addressed to the publisher.

ISBN 978 1 3982 5578 4

Designer: Sarah Bennett

British Library Cataloguing in Publication Data
A full catalogue record for this book is available from the British Library.

When a sunflower has finished blooming and its petals shrivel and brown, its head grows heavy with the weight of hundreds of seeds. Birds and small animals nibble at the seeds, knocking some down and carrying others far away. When the seeds find their way to the ground at last, they nestle into the soil and wait for winter to end.

A long time ago, in a beautiful city in Ukraine, a little girl named Tania lived in a cosy apartment with her mama and papa and babushka. While Mama and Papa worked at the hospital, Babushka took tender care of Tania. They read stories together for hours.

Babushka took Tania to the park to play and held her hand the whole way there. They marvelled at the cheerful sunflowers in bloom. Babushka explained how the seeds, safe in the centre of each blossom, would become flowers themselves the following year.

When Tania was six, a war began. She did not know what war was, only that it meant she and her mama and papa would have to leave home very suddenly. Their city was not safe any more.

The night Tania and her parents left, they had to leave behind almost everything, including Babushka, who was too old to travel.

There was only enough time for Mama to grab a handful of silver teaspoons from the drawer before they hurried away . . .

down the stairs . . .

across the city . . .

to the train that would take them to safety.

They had to keep moving to stay safe. They travelled from city to city, staying wherever they could find shelter. For a few nights, they slept in a theatre, like the one back home where Tania had taken ballet lessons. But they never stayed in one place for very long.

It scared Tania to hear military planes flying overhead and sirens in the distance. But they were safer on the move than they would be back home, Mama told her.

There was no school for Tania to go to. But Papa tutored her each evening, quizzing her in maths, science, geography and literature.

It was like this that Mama and Papa and Tania moved through day after day, night after night, waiting and hoping for the war to end.

When that day finally came, the air seemed easier to breathe, and the sun felt just a little warmer. But they could not go home. The war was over, but life would not be as it had been before.

Now Mama, Papa and Tania lived in a small town in a different country, far from their old city. The area was lined with long, low buildings, filled with other families who could not go home. Mama, Papa and Tania shared a single room, bare except for three small beds. No one knew for sure how long they would live in the little room – maybe for months, maybe for years.

How could a bare room ever feel like home? Tania wondered.

How could anywhere feel like home without Babushka?

It didn't feel like home. . . .

But some parts of life returned to normal. With the war over, Tania could finally go to school, and Mama and Papa could go to work. There was a rhythm to their days again.

Each afternoon after school, Tania curled up on her bed to read until Mama and Papa finished work.

One day, Papa came home with a few scraps of wood. Tania sat with her knees to her chest and watched him nail the wood together to make a simple shelf. Papa hung it on the wall, not too high so that Tania could still reach it. She carefully arranged their few books, lining up the spines just so with the edge of the shelf.

That winter, Mama filled her evenings with sewing. Whenever she could spare a moment, Mama pulled out her needle and thread. Little by little, her tiny, perfect stitches transformed some old flour sacks into crisp curtains and pillows.

One evening, when Mama had finished sewing, she hung the new curtains in the window. Papa pushed one of the beds against the wall under the bookshelf. Mama set the pillows in a row along the side of the bed to make it like a sofa.

By this time, their life before was a faraway heartache. It was hard to picture the old apartment. But Tania still remembered how it felt when Babushka tucked her in at night – like a little seed nestling into the soil.

One afternoon in early spring, Mama came home with a surprise – pysanky dye. She spread sunny yellow on the raw wooden floor until it glowed.

Then Tania and Papa watched from the sofa while Mama took a paintbrush to the window. Long green stems sprouted from the bottom of each curtain. Next, massive dark circles emerged from the stems. Finally, Mama surrounded each circle with glorious yellow blooms.

Satisfied, Mama came to rest next to Tania and Papa on the sofa. Tania closed her eyes. Now she could picture the window of the old apartment a little more clearly – Babushka's sunflowers peeking through, their faces turned hopefully towards the sun.

When Tania opened her eyes, she saw Mama's sunflowers at the window, smiling at them.

Tania smiled back.

AUTHOR'S NOTE

When Russia invaded Ukraine on 24 February 2022, I was struck by the images of children and their families packed onto train platforms, forced to flee without knowing exactly where they would go or when they might be able to return. My family and I thought immediately of my grandmother, Tatiana. She fled Ukraine with her parents in a very similar manner, almost 81 years before.

As people around the globe began responding to the modern Ukrainian refugee crisis in various ways, it seemed like sunflowers – the national flower of Ukraine and a symbol of hope – started cropping up everywhere. I remembered the story my grandmother told proudly, of how her mother brightened up their modest refugee housing with a little resourcefulness and cheerful images of sunflowers. Nana gave me her blessing to borrow the story, and the idea for this book was born.

A few words of acknowledgment: I am forever grateful to the entire team at Capstone, especially my brilliant editor, Kristen Mohn, for her endless patience and thoughtful, transformational edits; Olga Baumert and Sarah Bennett for the gorgeous art and design of this book; as well as Beth Brezenoff, Miriam Moore-Keish, and many others for believing that this story could be a real book and that I could be the one to author it.

Finally, I want to thank my grandmother for allowing me to tell this story, and my entire family for their unconditional love and support.

Readers may be wondering what happened to the "real" Mama, Papa and Tania. When my grandmother was 15, the family was sponsored by a church in Nebraska, USA, where they resettled. At that point, they had been away from their home in Kyiv for ten years, six of which were spent in temporary refugee housing, in the room with the painted sunflowers.

To be forced from one's home and separated from family is a life-changing trauma. The United Nations High Commissioner for Refugees estimates that there are currently around 27.1 million refugees in the world, or roughly the population of Australia. About half of these are children under 18, and more than two thirds of all refugees come from Syria, Venezuela, Afghanistan, South Sudan and Myanmar. My family and I hope that readers of this book will consider supporting displaced people around the world in whatever way they can. We also encourage you to look for signs of hope in your everyday surroundings, and if you don't see them, remember that you can create them!

Beatrice Rendón

ABOUT THE AUTHOR

Beatrice Rendón was born and raised in the United States. She has fond memories of her grandmother holding her hand, reading to her and tucking her in, just like Babushka and Tania in the story. Bea is a former teacher and a lifelong lover of children's literature. She studied educational policy and comparative religion at Macalester College and holds a Master of Arts in Teaching from Hamline University. She lives with her husband and their cat, Phoebe – named by the grandmother who inspired this book.

ABOUT THE ILLUSTRATOR

Originally from Poland, Olga Baumert studied fine art and jewellery-making before moving to the UK and earning a degree in graphic design and illustration from De Montfort University. Her art is inspired by great stories, interactions between people and nature, and open landscapes. Olga lives in Leicestershire, where she uses a mix of traditional techniques, including gouache, watercolour, acrylics and coloured pencils to make her art.